Make Time For You
(Every 90 Days)

Make Time For You
(Every 90 Days)

By

Linda Edith-Jacobs and Ron Whalen

authorHOUSE®

ISBN: 978-0-7596-0280-9 (sc)
ISBN: 978-0-7596-0279-3 (e)

Print information available on the last page.

This book is printed on acid free paper.

1stBooks - rev. 2/12/01

Congratulations! On your choice in selecting our book. "Make Time For You", is a book about choices in life.

The good news is, we all have choices. Some people may feel trapped or perhaps unaware of what choices are available to them.

As you continue to read this book, you will find that there are more choices for you than you think.

Have fun and be creative!

TIME IS FLYING BY...STOP?!

IT NEVER WILL.

DEDICATION

Always make time to give thanks to God first, because without Him we could not have accompolished the tasks to complete this book.

Enjoy prosperity whenever you can and when hard times come, understand that God shows you one side of the learning tree as well as the other. Nothing is for certain in this life. Nothing, except the love of God.

When the clouds are heavy, rain comes down. If you wait for perfect conditions, you will never get things done. Planning is the key! Keep sowing your seeds because you never know which will grow. Perhaps they all will.

We hope this book will help you to enjoy your life more; and with those you love.

To our children Dia, Kia and Ke'Ron.

To our grandchildren Joshua and Kayla.

To our parents Mary and Jacob; Ruth and Morris.

To our family, friends and the wonderful people we've met, who have shared their lives with us. Thank you!

Dedication (cont...)

Special Thanks To:

Kia Poindexter, Photographer

Dia Poindexter, Model

Ke'Ron Poindexter, Design

Kevin Barnett, Web Page Design

CONTENTS

Introduction xiii

Chapter

1. How To Take Control Of Your Life 1

2. Make Time For You 29

3. Key Items On How To Keep The Spotlight
    Shining On Your Relationship 47

4. Vacations 68

5. Setting Your Goals (The Plan) 74

6. Questions and Answers 80

7. How To Make Your Money Work For You .. 86

INTRODUCTION

Make Time For You highlights relationships and situations of couples with diverse life styles. The information we have compiled include young and older couples who have been in their relationship together for a continuous period of six months, up to fifty years.

A common goal they all shared was to maintain a healthy, happy relationship. To achieve that goal, the couples we spoke with said that you must first identify the problems or issues which could dissolve your relationship. Then your immediate course of action would be to not allow the problems to take over your life.

Make Time For You will reference some of the issues that could cause problems and point out how <u>you</u> could change or enhance your life and relationship through choices.

Make Time For You will not only talk about relationships and situations Involving couples, but, includes single individuals too! Our global message is about people and what they bring to the "table".

As an individual the goal of achieving a healthy, happy relationship with yourself is in your control. It is up to you to find the key to the door

of "inner peace and free spirit". It is your choice.

How To Take Control Of Your Life

Year after year we search for ways to free up our time for the things we want to do.

Each year we look back and wonder "where did all the time go?" Some people talk about exciting, fun vacations with family and friends, or a quiet romantic getaway for two. Other people take action and do it. They make time for vacations. They make time for family. They make time for each other. "What do you make time for?"

Our conversations with many different couples revealed to us that there is a common denomenator in the makings of a relationship. Each couple shared similar experiences that occurred at the beginning of their relationship and through out the dating period. What was common about the experience was that they spent a lot of time together doing different activities. They had fun! They looked forward to their next experience and were excited about getting together again! However, over a period of time their relationship changed, like charcoal in a barbecue grill that burns hot in the beginning and then slowly becomes cold as the charcoal burns out.

Similar changes occurred in their relationship, what they did not realize is that they could have controlled how the changes impacted their lives.

Think about it. You can prevent the charcoal from burning out by attending to its needs. Adding More charcoal will keep the grill hot!

Gradually, as time passed for these couples, doing different things together became infrequent. Spending less and less time together slowly became the "norm". For some, change occurred not really knowing that it was happening to them. For others, change occurred knowing it was happening, but they did nothing about it. A majority of the couples agreed after giving some thought about the course of their lives that it became an effort to make time for each other and even more of an effort to plan time to be alone

3

together. A common reason why relationships change is because of other demands. A choice we all have is <u>how</u> it changes. What became a reality for them was they were not able to squeeze in time for vacations or romantic getaways, therefore, these events did not happpened. Before they knew it years had passed. In retrospect, everything else (other demands) became more important than their relationship.

Unless you take control of the way you live your life, a cycle will continue and repeat over and over year after year. When you allow this type of cycle to continue you should not be surprised or disappointed when you become bored and tired of your life. You have choices!

It is not a secret that almost everything in our society wants our attention and manipulates our time. After all, that is how money is made, businessess profit, ratings are established, movie stars are created and how politics work. These demands that take over your life are a form of control. Control of your mind, control of your time and control of your future.

We have learned that as individuals we are empowered much more than we think.

Through planning, discipline and self motivation you could control how our society impact your life. Remember, "Just Say No".

The power of choice is within reach. You could choose to gradually make changes in your life or you could choose to make immediate changes in your life. If you choose to make an immediate change, do it now. Take your first step and begin today. Outline a plan, to *Make Time For You.* Use our easy to follow steps to help get you started.

Fifteen years ago we took our steps and decided to make time together every 90 days! Wanting to travel and see different parts of the world was a childhood dream we both shared. One of many exciting moments in our relationship was that we made it possible to fullfill that dream. Over the fifteen years we have traveled to Hawaii, the Pyramids of Giza, cruised the Carribbean and stood on the Island of Mayo. We have seen strange activity across the ocean that looked like lighting, as we traveled through the Bermuda Triangle. The travel experiences are a part of what we have shared together. Not only was it fun but educational too!

To have the opportunity to learn and have fun all at the same time is what this tree of life is all about. When you achieve a goal you have set for yourself it feels wonderful. That is why it is important for us to let you know that we have accompolished some of our personal goals even while raising a family. That alone may seem impossible, but in addition to achieving some of our personal goals and raising a family, we are working people too! Surprise, surprise!?

People are very surprised when we tell them that we are working people with a family. They want to know how is it possible? Some reactions have been, "you guys must be rich or inherited money from a relative". They generally would say that there is no way you could travel like that when you have everyday living expenses and especially with children. It is not possible. The common question then follows. "How do you find the time?"

We are here to tell you that it was possible and it is possible because we followed the guidelines outlined in this book. We took the steps because we were inspired by the last spoken words of a mother to her son before she past away. She said, *"Son, do not wait until you retire to enjoy your wife".*

From that moment on we began our steps. We set up our plan of action and applied dicipline to our life. We make everyday count because we realized this was time we could not get back.

9

"Time is passing by...stop?! It never will". This is a quote from a poem written by a family member. It expresses so clearly the message we want you to get from this book.

When you take no action you get no results. The facts are, the amount of time you have for yourself and your loved ones is limited. The majority of your time is in demand and manipulated by the system. You use up a lot of energy trying to gain control of your day.

Let's look at some general statistics on the way your time maybe manipulated (the

numbers here represent the "system"): **365 - 10 - 100 = 255.**

What the numbers mean is that, there are three hundred sixty five days (365) in a year, ten days of vacation time and 100 weekend days also, within a one year window.

It is reasonable to say that within a twelve month period, people have two weeks of vacation time. They would usually take one week at a time mainly to stretch their days off throughout the year.

Weekends are a total of two (2) days off , we have included these days in this example. We are not assuming that everyone have weekends off. However, to make this point let's say you work a

Monday through Friday job and that you have weekends off.

After taking a closer look at these numbers you begin to realize that out of **365 days** in a year, a two week vacation adds up to **10 days** and your weekend time off adds up to **100 days.** Your total number of days off in a year's time is only **110 days**. One hundred and ten days may sound like a lot of time but when you look at the big picture the vaction time is usually taken one week at a time during a particular season such as Fall, Winter or Spring reserving the other week for time off during the Summer season. In other cases people would break up their vacation time taking a day here and a day there trying to spread their time off over the year. The weekend time of 100 days is taken in **2 day** increments, often this time is used to play "catch up", usually for the things you can't get done during the week. You also try to have some fun and maybe get a little rest too!

Is'nt it funny that you have it all planned in your head how things are going to go but when you think back to last weekend it did not happen at all as you had planned it. Then you begin to think about previous weekends and even back to the previous year and question why you did not accomplish some of the things you wanted to do. You also begin to realize that one hundred and ten days is not a lot of time and that the number of days allowed for you within a twelve month window are not being defined by you.

The point we are making is that the scale is one sided. There is no balance between the demands on your time and the time allowed for you. It is not by accident that you are stressed, unable to make time for a family vacation or a romantic getaway. Do not let another year go by only to look back and wonder, "where did all the time go." Take control of your life. Make Time For You. Use your vacation time to truly relax. Take a break from the routine. Your mind and body will love you for it!!

Understand that there are demands in your life that you <u>can</u> control and demands that you <u>cannot</u> control.

Some of the demands you have control over are work, school and social activities. We will talk more about those further on in the book.

Some of the demands we have <u>no</u> control over are listed below. As stated earlier any demand creates change in your life. We encourage you to challenge your thoughts when you confront what to do and how you would go about doing it when you are faced with a situation you have no control over.

Here are some situations we have no control over:

* Accidents   * Death (in the Family)

* Illness   * Weather Conditions

* Vehicle Problems

These situations force you to make immediate adjustments to your routine. Guess What? You adjust to them too! Stop and think about this a moment. You live through it, you make arrangements, you re-adjust, you change up for however long it takes or is neccessary for you to get beyond that point and most importantly you get through it!

If you can adjust to unexpected situations which interrupt the routine in your life and you still follow through with the demands of work, school, and social activities, **can you adjust your life to make time for you?**

Yes you can! Here's how:

Get yourself a calendar, an ink pen and some markers. Get the kind of markers used for highlighting.

In the memorandum section or a blank space on your calendar, list five (5) short term personal goals. If your calendar does not have space to write, use a note pad. The reason we suggest a calender to list your ideas on is because it is visible and usually looked at frequently. And as a visual society, this is sort of the "in your face approach".

What are some personal goals you have wanted to accomplish? They do not have to be major projects. It is usually the little things that make a big difference. When you have listed your five (5) personal goals, the next step is to prioritize the list. Number your goals one through five with one being your top priority and so-on. Take your marker and highlight the first goal Let us say your first goal is a romantic getaway, something you have been wanting to do for a while but just could not find the time. The next step is to make it happen.

A number of people might freeze up and stop at this point because you are not quite sure what to do next. It is okay, just do not be discouraged. Be creative with your thoughts. This is generally the most difficult step and you are not alone. This is one of the elements you need to identify. You need to confront it and then take control. You may feel overwhelmed, trapped, locked into your day-to-day routine or simply do not know how to fit this goal into your schedule. To make it happen and succeed with your goals is really not as difficult as you may think. All you need is a plan.

When you outline a plan you create a beginning and an end. This is your time frame to achieve that goal in. It is very important to be realistic and honest with yourself when setting your time frames. Avoid pressure on you and more importantly, do not set yourself up for failure. Look at your calendar and choose a month and a date. This is your beginning. To get you started with your next step think about what this popular phrase is saying to you..."Today is the first day of the rest of your life". With that thought in mind we encourage you to start with today's date to establish your beginning.

We also, encourage you to walk through these steps with us just to see how easy they are to follow.

Use the marker to make a **left** bracket ([ ) around today's date on your calendar. Count thirty (30) days forward and make a **right** bracket ( ]) on day thirty (30). Select a day between the brackets. CIRCLE THAT DAY! The day that you choose will be the time for your romantic getaway. This is "YOUR TIME"!! Enjoy this time however you choose.

If you feel like something is holding you back, ask yourself why? Compare your reasons with the ones that are listed below. These are quotes from people who have shared their thoughts and feelings with us.

- "I feel guilty spending money on myself, besides, what would I do!?"

- "Right now we can't get away, we work different hours. We just don't have the time".

- It took us a long time to build up our savings account; we don't want to touch it now".

- "We don't have anyone to watch the kids".

- Do you have similar thoughts and feelings? If so, consider for a moment the following:

- You spend money on "material things".

- You give your time and energy for "others".

- You make time for work related functions.

- You make time for volunteer/community activities.

- Why not give some time to you?

When you make time for yourself you establish a balance in your life. It is very important that you have balance in your life to level out the amount of energy you use to keep up with the different directions you take in the course of a day. The end results when its time to give to yourself or to your relationship is an unbalanced scale. You are just too tired! When you function on a one sided scale, like a hot Pressure Cooker at maximum temperature, if you release the lid just a little, all h... breaks loose.

You deserve some special attention. It's good for the mind, it's good for the body and it's good for the soul. Enjoy some of the pleasures of life. "Grab yourself a cup of Chicken Noodle Soup." Treat yourself to a hot sauna or candlelight dinner for two. You could go to a movie matinee during the day, followed by a romantic evening. Purchase a round-trip ticket either by train or bus, to an exciting destination for the day. The choice of transportation is up to you and whatever type of experience you want to explore.

You could plan and enjoy the activities as a couple, as a single person, with or without children. All you need to do is plan ahead. Use the day that you select for your time and your time only!

Take Control, use these steps to help motivate you to begin doing the things you <u>think</u> you do not have time for.

Congratulations! On your choice, to <u>Take</u> <u>Control Of Your Life</u>.

Make Time For You

There are "passing" comments that occur when you meet people for the first time no matter who they are or where they are from. Comments about the weather, about a current event or about a recent movie. These are generally "safe" topics. However, when you meet people for the first time and your meeting arrangement is for a longer period of time, perhaps dinner together or at a social gathering; the conversation evolves to more specific and personable topics. A popular topic for discussion is how hard it is to make time for yourself, expecially when there are too many demands.

We kept a diary of the conversations we had with different people during our travels over the years. It became obvious to us that people genuinely felt they had very little time for their own personal nurturing. However, we heard the opposite from different couples who have been in their relationship for a long period of time. It was obvious that for them, making time for each other and nurturing their relationship was important. It was also inspiring for us to see and feel the joy of two people who have traveled a long road together "hand-in-hand".

You must allow time for you to nurture the mind and the body. Give yourself what we call an **"Inner Tuning"**.

As you take these steps you are certain to find your key that will open the door to a healthier, happier you.

Listed below are thoughts and feelings that were shared by people who may be experiencing the same things you are.

a) "I just don't have the time to do the things I want to do".

b) "We use to do things together and it was fun; but now we don't have the time, we're both too busy".

c) "This is the first time in eight years, since the children were born, that my husban and I could go somewhere together without them".

d) "Our relationship has changed. The things we did together were different when we first met compared to now".

e) "The cost of living is too high. Who can afford to do anything today? We're barely making ends meet".

f) "I'm not sure how to build a relationship, it was never taught to me when I was growing up.

g) "After the children were born my wife and I sort of let ourselves go, and now we feel unattractive".

h) "We put our money into building our
home. We don't have any to spend on
us".

The statements listed above are a few of the
elements that have dissolved relationships over a
period of time. Why? Because the focus in the
relationship had changed.

In the beginning of the relationship their
attention and energy was on each other. As time
passed, the focus disolved into the situations
detailed in the above statements (a through h).

If these situations describe your relationship either in part or whole and you feel stuck or trapped, try the following choices:

1. <u>**Act On Positive Thoughts:**</u>

To act on your thoughts simply mean doing what you think about. For example, you may have thought about a romantic getaway with your partner, or how nice it would be for the two of you to have some time together in the perfect setting. Perhaps, lately you've been thinking about the fun you use to have when you did do things together.

You may have even talked about what you use to do together, a long time ago! You both smile, then hesitate, but finally conclude, that these things happened when you were younger. You both end the conversation without really wanting too because there is more you want to talk about. The conversation ends like the flip of a switch turning off the lights to your memories. Your thoughts return to the current issues and you go on about your business. The cycle begins. Not so fast! Flip the memory switch back on, because these are the positive thoughts we are talking about. This is the time to actually take those thoughts a step further.

Ask your partner to go out on a date with you , then have some fun planning it. We encourage you to not just think the thoughts or talk about what you use to do; but rather to take action, take control and do it.

2. Identify And Make A List Of The Things You Want To Accomplish:

The easiest way, is to randomly list your ideas as they come up. This action could be done over a period of time, no pressure, just add to your list when the ideas come to mind. You could prioritize them at a later time.

Here are some examples:

Instead of sitting in front of the television after dinner, take a walk. Schedule your walk time for two days a week. Mark the days and time of the walk on your calendar. Set a start and end date. The time frame would help you to build a routine and by sticking to the routine it would help you to achieve your goal. When was the last time you visited a museum? If this is an activity you like to do, **PLAN IT and DO IT!**

Here's how:

Get your calendar and a different color highlighter. When you look back over your calendar you could quickly identify your activities by the choice of colors you used. We are a visual society, so coordinating the colors really helps it adds creativity and it is fun too! Plan your trip using the same steps as before. This activity requires minimal planning. Schedule the trip to allow you a comfortable amount of time to make the necessary arrangements depending upon your situation. Select your time frame for this trip. The time frame could be within 30, 60 or 90 days. You should choose the best time for you. For this example we will choose a 90 days window.

Select your start date, make a **left** bracket ([ ) on your calendar, this is day one. Count 90 days forward and a make a **right** bracket ( ]) on day 90. Select a day between the brackets and circle that day! This is the day of your trip.

3. <u>Make Decisions Together and Apply Discipline:</u>

Here is where the fun ignites. Split the planning arrangements between you and your partner. This applies to married couples, dating couples or single people, whatever! Outline the tasks together, then either pick, assign or voluntare for the responsibilites you both will follow up on. One could research types of museums you want to visit, where they are located, what hours they are open, find out if there are special events coming and what the cost would be. The other could research a cost effective way to travel, find out if it is to your advantage to travel by car, by train or by bus. If you travel by train or bus get a list of the departure and arrival times. The list will provide you with choices during the planning stage.

4. <u>Plan Ahead And Follow Through:</u>

You would be amazed at how inexpensive long distance travel could be when you plan ahead. We spent under $500.00 for two roundtrip airplane tickets from Connecticut to Los Angeles, California to surprise a family member for his 50th birthday. That was a pretty good deal! There are other low travel rates with Five Star quality "out there." Take advantage.

Arrangements for children to stay with grandparents or an aunt and uncle could be a challenge. You have to plan your trip around two households. That too, could be fun with the right approach. If family members do not live near by, plan your getaway trip destination in the surrounding area to where they live. The children would be dropped off on your way to the getaway destination and picked up on your way back home. If you do not have children this is a step you could skip. Additional arrangements include, coordinating meals for the two of you. If you want to avoid the the cost of expensive restaurants, bring a picnic basket with prepared food from home. On one of the family trips we brought our small microwave oven with us to heat food we pre-cooked for the trip. We had delicious home cooked meals away from home. In addition, we minimized our travel expenses because we did not have to eat out at restaurants daily. Be creative with your ideas, you could "dress up your plans, or dress them down." The choice is yours!

5. **Within The Next Thirty Days Make Changes In Your Life. If You Think About Doing Something Positive, Do It!:**

Begin your steps today. It was twenty years ago for us and that time has gone by so quickly.

As you struggle through your day to day activities, know that the clock is always ticking.

Time is flying by.....Stop?!....It never will.

You <u>will</u> wake up one morning to find that thirty (30) days have gone by. Time is truly precious. It is not promised to anyone. Look up and see beyond what is immediately in front of you. You have the power of choice. Make a difference in your life and you will help make a difference for someone else.

Outline a plan today! Make it visible! If you could see it and touch it, then must be real. Right? Make it happen.

Linda Edith Jacobs and Ron Whalen

Congratulations…On your choice to <u>Make Time</u> and Do It!

Key Items On How To Keep

The Spotlight Shining On Your Relationship

There are a number of key items that keep the spotlight shining on a relationship. Outlined below are only five of the Key Items we have covered. There are more.:

1) <u>Share Quality Time Together:</u>

A Relationship involves individuals with different ideas and thoughts. By sharing your ideas, thoughts and activities with each other you would add diversity to your relationship and would make life more interesting for the other.

47

To share, you have to first make time for each other. Many couples grow apart because they allow outside elements to come between them.

Examples:

In the work place, an eight (8) hours a day job can extend to eleven/twelve hours a day with meetings, community involvement activities, even traveling to and from work or work related functions.

Social activities taken to the extreme could also cause strain in a relationship too! If one or both of you play a team sport, such as, basketball, tennis, bowling. In addition to your work time out of the house, you're also out of the house one or two nights a week for your sport activity. During the peak season your two nights a week for practice becomes four nights a week, plus weekends for the games. What happens is you and your partner spend less and less time together. As we all know time never stops and before you know it, while you and your partner are spending less time together you are both changing. This is okay, because life is about change. The reality is regardless of your initial plans you both will change with or without the other around. Time will do that too! What could ultimately happen, if you let it, is that you could grow apart from each other and not together.

Couples could grow apart because they do not Make Time to share with each other and as time passes their interests change. You can't stop time, but you do have choices.

2. Plan For What You Want:

Plan and celebrate time together because you want to, because it means something to you. Not because the date on the calendar is valentine's day and you feel obligated to do something for each other. Be together and plan time with your partner because it is special for you and it comes from your heart. Special moments feel special in your heart when guided by your emotions. Not when your emotions are manipulated and your actions are controlled because of expectations or that you feel obligated.

There are overwhelming demands in our society that manipulate and control how you should think and how you should feel. If you don't live up to the expectations or demands you are made to feel bad inside, in some cases you are excluded and isolated too! Then you react because you feel you have too and not just because you feel you have too, but because you want to be included and be liked by others.

Examples:

a) On Valentine's day you send a card, flowers or candy to loved ones.

b) On Easter you get a card or an Easter basket for someone.

c) You send mother/father day cards on the designated days.

These actions may not be what you truly feel but you do them anyway. Because if you don't, well, what would people think?

Our message to you is to let all of that "stuff" go! Be who you are and share who you are inside.

Keep the spotlight shining on your relationship by taking control of your own life.

Communicate with each other. Share your thoughts, ideas and emotions openly. It is important to understand and accept that you are both individuals. What one person may think, may not occur to the other.

If you feel like sending flowers because you want the person to know you are thinking about them. Do it! Do it because it is a feeling <u>you</u> have at that moment. Do not force yourself to do something because other people are doing it. If in your heart right now, you would like to write a note or send a greeting card to share your thoughts with someone you love or with a friend. Do it!! Do it at the moment, because the words are fresh in your mind and the feeling has filled your heart. Do it, before you loose the moment. Thoughts are like flash cards, they pass through your mind quickly. No one will know how you are feeling unless you share those feelings. It is not always easy to verbally express what we feel inside. Some people find ways to <u>show</u> how they feel.

Being in touch with your feelings, the real self, makes you unique. That is why it is important to share your feelings as they surface, if you do not, time passes and you loose the moment.

How many people you know spend a lot of time talking about what they wish, they should have, could have done?

3. <u>Respect Each Others Thoughts and Ideas:</u>

The words stated above should be easy to follow and understand. Yes? No! There are different interpretations on what it means to respect each others thoughts and ideas. Relationships involve individuals with differences.

Have you ever wondered why your parents, your religion, dictated a set of rules for you to follow as you were growing up?

It is generally because people are afraid of the "unknown." People are also afraid of the truth. It is because of fear, people have made up stories and twisted the truth. These actions have kept distance between groups of people for generations. The wonderful reality about our universe that has kept the human spirit in forward motion, is that life survives on differences.

Human differences have influenced change in our society throughout history. If you study the changes closely you may begin to understand why it is difficult for people to share who they really are. What we are taught by traditional methods and what the spiritual lessons teach us, are mixed messages. A common reason, is that people want to be accepted. However, to be accepted, you have to live up to the expectations created by the "system".

If you stop and think about what is really happening to you, you will learn that a lot of your time and energy is spent on trying to fit into a mold that does not fit. After years of pretending to be who you are not, you loose touch with your individuality and self identity.

If you are existing under conditions like these, how could you have an honest relationship and how do you feel good about yourself?

Make Time For You, encourages you to focus on your "Inner Tuning". Embrace the spirit and beauty of life. Allow your creativity to flow, then share your talent. Communicate openly with your partner. Choose topics on different subjects and talk about them, including your relationship.

Structure your relationship so that you both could grow. Would it be interesting if an idea of yours, combined with an idea of your partner, turns out to a master plan?

4. <u>Friendship:</u>

What does friendship mean to you? How is it defined in the dictionary? Look it up and compare it with your own definition.

What friendship means to you, could be very different to your partner. The first step towards building a friendship is to communicate. This also is true with starting a relationship. With any type of long term relationship, you need trust, support and a special bond to build a strong foundation.

Open two-way communication with your partner gives him or her a choice on how to handle a situation or the elements that may occurr in the relationship. When you manipulate the truth to avoid confrontation or to obtain control, whatever your individual reasons are, you tamper with the foundation of what your relationship was built on. Trust and support!

As a team, on the top of your list should be, do not take each other for granted. What could happen over time, is that you begin to feel trapped in the relationship because one person choose to think for the both of you.

Do not be fooled, there are no perfect human beings. "We are all going to make mistakes along the way. Do not confuse making a mistake with an excuse. A mistake is something you do, not knowing the outcome. An excuse is something you do, knowing the potential outcome, but said it was a mistake when you get caught. You know, like the President.

In any event, the point we are making is that you could control the direction of your relationship through choices!

5. Romantic Getaways:

Romantic getaways are special times together for couples. It is an extension of dating. A time to experience the excitement again of your first date and the passion of your first kiss.

A majority of the couples who have been together ten years or longer shared with us that they have more fun together now, then they did at the beginning of their relationship. The secret is time! Over a period of time they had developed a level of comfort and trust to explore each other more intimately without the limits of fear.

❶ Are you comfortable with your partner?

❷ Do you have romantic getaways together?

If your answers are no to the questions above, find a quiet spot right now and answer the questions below:

❶ <u>When</u> did the romance of dating end in your relationship?

❷ <u>Why</u> did the romantic times together end?

If you do not know the answer or don't have a clue, never even gave it a thought, there could be a problem brewing in your relationship. No romance, and no communication are some of the elements that could dissolve your relationship. A majority of the couples we spoke with had a common reply when asked, "what was the one thing that was always on your mind before the two of you got married?" The reply was, "looking forward to our next date and looking forward to being together again".

When they were not together all they could think about was each other. The romance, the hugs, the laughter you both shared are real open emotions that ignited your relationship.

When you suppress or ignore these feelings the relationship could change. The longer you stay together in a healthy, happy relationship, a special bond occurs between the two of you over the years. Your relationship becomes stronger because your love and trust for each other grows.. You grow as individuals when you respect each others differences and encourage them to flourish. You grow as a team when you encourage each others growth.

The secret to happiness that so many people are in search of, is really not a secret. The main ingredients have been outlined for you in this book. All you need to do is make time and try it!! Try living life, instead of just existing. Try feeling life, instead of just seeing it, like a little child in a toy store, "I want, I want, I want," everything that they see they want and when you bring it home, it sits un-touched. Make Time For You is about choices. Work on growing your relationship. Plan trips together with and without the children.

Romantic Getaways means to date each other again and again and again. Think of your relationship as a living thing, you must nurture it, for it to grow!

Congratulatioins...On your choice to <u>Keep The</u>

<u>Spotlight Shining On Your Relationship!</u>

Vacations

Imagine working eight hours a day, five days a week. You come home only to conquer another challenge. That challenge could be children, school, community activities even house chores.

Let us focus on children. Parenting is a special skill, that gets very little credit or recognition in our society. First and foremost you must be able to multi-task as a parent. Children need for you to take them to their after school activities, to the doctors, and for some people, to and from school. They need for you to take them to a friends house, to come to the parents night, to take them here and there. They need new sneakers for their basketball, volleyball, softball games or for their cheerleader competition. In short, they need your time!

When you are through taking care of there needs, you prepare dinner, clean up and then get ready for the next day before colasping in bed. What a long day! You think to yourself, I need a break and about how or when you could take a break. You wonder how do other people do it.

For us, as we mentioned earlier, we do it by following the steps in this book. People who take vacations benefit in several ways. They take time to relax, reconnect with their spouse which in most busy households is hard to do because of the different directions you both are going. People who take vacations, take control of their lives, even if it is for a short period of time. The main focus is that when you are in control you have the options to create or surround yourself in an atmosphere of your choice.

Your choice may be a vacation to relax, to move at your own pace, read a book without interruption, to curl up on your couch and watch a good movie or sit in a room alone and listen to soothing music. To meditate by the ocean and watch the waves gently climb the shore.

Some people choose vacations that are adventurous and busy. They plan exciting trips to the ancient Pyramids, they explore the wonders of the world, or go scuba diving in search of some lost caves.

Whatever the choice may be, during your vacations you could pamper your body. Get a message and sit in a soothing hot tub or jacuzzi...ummmmmm! You could try a manicure,pedicure or a facial. Try an aerobic workout or a yoga class, you will find that these activities help the body free itself from everyday stress and is refreshing for the soul.

Connecting with your partner is so very important and is the biggest benefit in taking vacations. You could set it up to have quality time together. To be able to talk and listen to each other without interruptions.

It is always nice to have dinner over candlelight, you could talk about different interests, about the future. The conversation could be about anything, the important message and the point we are making, is that you are focused on each other. Life is a big responsibility. It can get pretty stressful, expecially when you don't take the time to "let down".

Take time, to make time!

Congratulations...On your choice to make <u>Vacation</u> time for you!

Setting Your Goals (The Plan)

We all have different motivators but we all need a plan to achieve our goals.

Once you have decided on what you want to do, write down your plan. Outline the idea in an easy to follow format. This creates the steps toward reaching your goals. You have made your goal visible to you, rather than leaving it in your thoughts.

If you can see it, then it must be real.

You now have a plan that you can see and control as you create each step.

Always remember, it is the little things that make the biggest difference. Do not set yourself up for failure. Focus on the things that you know you are capable of doing. Develop the diciplines, then expand your goals.

When you are planning your vacations make sure you avoid the potential stress, like the things you need to do around the house before you go on your trip. Some of the things you may want to take care of prior to your trip are:

❶ Pay the bills that will come due while you are away.

❷ Schedule your doctors visit according to your medical needs

❸ Unplug your stereo, tv and electrical kitchen appliances.

❹ If you are traveling during the colder months, make sure your heat is on low to keep the pipes from freezing.

❺ Notify the post office to hold your mail (if necessary).

❻ Do not forget to return the video rentals back to the video store.

❼ Mow your lawn. For some people mowing the lawn is stressful. It would be double the work when you return, because now the grass is thicker and if it rained, the grass is wet too! Returning from a wonderful vaction, to cut grass along with your other chores, is not exactly an ideal choice. You want to savor the end of your vacation for time to reflect on the moments and the experience together. Allow yourself to gradually transition back in to your routine. You could use the end of your vaction time to share photographs or a video of the trip with family or friends.

These are some examples of how planning ahead could work for you. The point is, you have options! Planning is key and it works! When you have a plan and it is visible to you, the steps are easier and the direction you are going is in your control.

Think of your plan as a road map. To get to your destination, you must plot the course and prepare for the trip. If you do not plan or prepare, getting to your destination could be frustrating and time consuming. You could end up driving around in circles. Make a difference in your life through planning. Get your calendar, your markers and set your goals. Make time for you and make time for your family.

Congratulations!...On Setting You Goals (The Plan).

Questions and Answers

Here are some general questions and answers that have helped couples in their relationship as well as individuals to begin a relationship:

1. <u>How do you make the time?</u>

You make time for yourself the same way you make time for everything else you do. Through planning and committment. Organize your personal life as you would in your work environment using Time Management. When you set up a schedule and plan your day, week, month and year. You immediately gain control of your life.

2. <u>What can you do?</u>

What you can do right now is make a list of goals you want to work towards. Create your list by writing them down randomly as they flow from your thoughts. When your list is complete, look it over and put a time frame next to each goal. Be realistic with yourself when setting your time frame. Again, it is very important not to set a time frame that can not be met!

Highlight the goals you feel have the shortest time frame. It is always encouraging and definitely motivating when you experience your results sooner than later! Use the same steps outlined on prior pages using your marker and your calendar to make your goals a reality.

Your true success is when you achieve the goals you have planned.

3. <u>How can you achieve your goals?</u>

The answer to this question is easy and really very simple. It is, however, the hardest step to follow.

To achieve your goals you would need to apply:

a) Discipline

b) Planning

c) Follow Through

4. <u>What about money?</u>

What <u>about</u> money? Money is only a tool! The first plan of action is to change the way you think about money. Let your money work for <u>you</u>, instead of <u>you</u> working for your money! Use money as the tool that it is. You do not have to make a lot of money to achieve your goals. It is not about how much money you make, it is about how you spend your money.

Up to now you have learned:

☺ **How To Take Control Of Your Life**

☺ **Steps In Making Time For You**

☺ **Key Items On How To Keep The Spotlight Shinning On Your Relationship**

☺ **Questions and Answers (On What You Can Do To Make A Change)**

The next step is: Cash Flow!

How To Make Your Money Work For You

Take charge of how you use your money. Restructure how you distribute your money!! Be specific and be consistent.

When you are specific with your money you can account for where your dollars go. When you are consistent with your money time will show the results. There are constant demands on your earned dollars. You know them as taxes. Look over your next pay stub at some common deductions:

☺ - Fed Tax

☺ - FICA

☺ - State Tax

☺ - Life Ins

☺ - Disability Ins

☺ - Social Security

☺ - Medical Ins

These deductions are part of the situations that exist in our society. Find out what your minimal deduction options are. Make sure that your standard deductions are the amounts required to avoid having to pay back taxes. Consult with an Accountant regarding your individual financial status.

After the standard deductions are subtracted from your gross pay, you have the net dollars to work with. Use your net dollars when calculating and planning time for you.

Here are some tips on ways to restructure and distribute your money, including ways to save for your romantic getaways!

There are four months in the year with five weeks. Identify these months on the calendar using your marker to highlight them. The remaining eight months in the year have four weeks each. Since the eight months are the majority number of months in the year, structure your living arrangements around the eight months with the four weeks. We will refer to these months as the, "four week plan".

To structure your living arrangements with the "four week plan" add up your monthly expense and then add up your monthly income. Your monthly income must be higher than your monthly expense. If not, then you need to earn additional income for this plan to work. For those of you who are paid weekly, you could allocate the appropriate dollar amount out of all four checks to pay the bills. During the months with five weeks, your fifth week's pay-check is money you could save. The reason this is money you could save, is because your monthly expenses are being paid by the "four week plan". That makes the fifth check extra income! The months that you receive five pay checks, save the fifth check.

Take the fifth week's pay and place it in an envelope. Seal it and label it with the date of your trip.

For the people who are paid bi-weekly, split your monthly bills and allocate payment out of the two pay checks received each month. There are months in the year where you will receive three pay-checks. Identify those months on your calendar and highlight them.

The months that you receive three pay checks, save the third check. Seal it in your special savings envelope and write the date of your trip on it. Other resources to make money work for you are:

☺ Quit smoking - If you are a smoker and have recently quit, save the money that you would have spent to purchase cigarettes. When you calculate how much was spent, these are the results. Let us say you smoked a pack of cigarettes a day, the cost for a pack of cigarettes are $3.00. You would spend approximately $84.00 (tax not included) a month. Multiply $84.00 x 3 months. Your savings would total $252.00. This is money that could work for you!

⏱ <u>Overtime</u> - This is another way to get additional income. It is important to plan that when you work overtime, what you will use the money for. Overtime should be money used for something <u>you</u> want to do. Leave you monthly bills to your "four week plan" option. When you use all of your money to pay bills, what generally happens is that you use the credit card for recreation. Then you become depressed when the bill comes in and you have to pay it back. The goal is to plan ahead and save your money for your activities. When you do use your credit card set aside the amount of what you plan to charge and be ready to pay it back when the bill arrives. You could also choose to make your scheduled payments on the bill with the money you have already saved. This option is especially beneficial if you are working on building your credit history.

☺ <u>Part time job</u> - In addition to your full time employment a part time job could be useful to catch up on some over spending you have done. The goal here is to calculate in advance how much income you would need to make from your part-time job, including the time frame required to obtain it. Use your marker and place brackets on the calendar to show the time frame. Let us say three months (90 days) will be enough time to accomplish this goal. At the end of the three months period you could terminate your employment from the part time job. Another choice you may consider is, instead of leaving your part time job after your bills are caught up, continue the part time work for an additional month or two. Take the money you earned and reward yourself with a fabulous fun activity for sticking to your goal! Most part time jobs are four or five hours a day. The pay is generally minimum wage of $5.10 per hour. The pay adds up to look like this: 4 x $5.10 = $20.40 a day x 5 days = $101.20 a week. In three months time you have earned $1,244.40.

⊕ <u>Income tax refunds</u> - is money returned to you each year. If you have followed the steps outlined in this book, your income tax check should be additional money. Use some or all of it towards your romantic getaway for the two of you.

⊕ <u>Raise or Promotion</u>...should also be additional money not yet included in your "four week plan". Once again reward yourself! You've earned it!

⊕ <u>Savings</u> - accounts are another tool to use. You and your partner decide on a dollar amount each would save per pay check. Then stick too it! Establish your time frame this money will be used for. Outline your start and end date on your calendar and go for it!

To make money work for you, take control of how you use your dollars. Avoid spending more than what you earn. The more debt you get yourself into, the less control you have.

Let's say your monthly bills total $1884.00 and your net income is $2084.00 a month. Your best friend or a neighbor just bought a brand new car and talked you into doing the same. The new car will cost you $350.00 more a month. Now your monthly bills total $2234.00 but your income remains the same.

You are spending more, than what you earn.

Here is an example of a couple who receives excellent benefits from their employer but does not have control or a plan on how they spend their money. They shared the same response we have received from other couples. They feel as though they do not have the time or the money to take vacations together and they eagerly want to make time for each other.

They both work at a casino as blackjack dealers and receive excellent benefits. The average salary for a blackjack dealer is $15.00 an hour with an annual bonus of $1,000.00 for a full-time dealer, $500.00 for a part-time dealer and a $200.00 bonus for a casual dealer.

Medical coverage include a low co-payment of $10.00 per doctor visits. Physicals are free and prescriptions are free when purchased at the pharmacy on the reservation. Dental insurance pays 80% of all dental visits.

Other benefits includes discounted meal tickets, discounts for shows, salons, and all stores on the reservation. These are great benefits! This couple could take a romatic getaway every 90 days with no problem, but they can not afford it!

However, if they followed the steps outlined in this book, and take advantage of the resources available to them they would be able to make time for each other and gain more control over their expenses. A majority of the people we have talked with said that they would love to go on a romantic getaway vacation every 90 days. When we shared

the 90 days calendar plan with them and showed

them how they could have exciting times together

with that special someone every 90 days and still

have their two weeks vacations each year. The

room grew brighter from the big smiles that

stretched across their face and the huge eyeballs

that opened wide. People who are very set in to

their routine have asked why should they change,

they are making ends meet. These are the same

people who have become bored with lives and feel

trapped.

It was the day before New Years Eve, while

using the bathroom in a public facility, the voice

in the next stall spoke. The initial comments were about the weather (it was cold) and what the conditions were going to be on New Years Eve (the weather report said freezing rain). This person then began to talk about personal feelings pertaining to her relationship.

The voice said that she and her husban have not gone out for New Years Eve in 20 years. She talked about the fun she had, the beautiful evening gown that she wore and the music of the big band that played. She talked of that night as though it was just last year, that she went out for New Years. Then her voice changed when she said, "I do not have to worry about driving in that weather, my husban is going to be sitting in front of the TV like he does every year, watching football." She took a deep sigh and said "I could have pushed the issue and did something about it over the years, I guess I just allowed it to happened." She really did want to go out for New Years, despite the weather conditions.

What was remembered most about this conversation was how lives are impacted. It was obvious that the feelings this person had was tucked safely in her memory but the yearning to have that feeling again was always just under the surfaced. What were the elements that kept them from sharing moments like the New Years Eve party 20 years ago? What stopped them from sharing these moments over and over again? Was it money?

Learn how to take control of your life. The sooner you learn, the more choices you will have.

Money problems could add pressure to a relationship. However, money is a controllable element.

Take control of your actions. Your relationship would be more healthier and happier too!

Remember we all have choices, we just need to know what they are:

❶ Take your partner out to a movie or to dinner.

❷ Make a picnic basket and go to a museum or a park.

❸ Try an activity that is new to the both of you.

❹ Explore something different together.

❺ Take a trip and share the planning.

❻ Arrange for the children to stay over your parents or at their aunt and uncle's house and share a relaxing romantic evening home together.

❼ Work on a project together that the two of you like doing.

The point is, <u>make time</u> for each other. If your finances are very tight at the moment, enjoy fun evenings at home alone. Create your own theme! That works too!

If you include these choices in your life, you would soon learn that you too could enjoy romantic getaways every 90 days.

Have fun with your planning and enjoy the comforts of being in control of your life.

Make **T**ime **F**or **Y**ou, is about choices.

ABOUT THE AUTHOR

Using their own experiences as individuals, as a couple, and as parents Ron and Linda take you through some of the planning in their lives that will provide the tools you will need to *Make Time For You*!

They do not claim to be experts, only that as common working class people, what they have done together, worked!

Their inspiration for this book came from many sources including the people they have met during their travels over the years. But the real reason for the change in their lives was when Ron's mother became sick and the words she spoke before she died. She told him that we (people) do not have a lot of time on earth and what little time we do have goes by fast. She told her son to take the time to make time for him and his wife.

The first order of business for Ron and Linda was the planning. From that moment to this moment (20 years later) they have shared positive values, productive lifestyles, lots of fun and exciting adventures together.

This book was written to help you to understand that it is how **you** think, that controls **you**. Thinking is power and for Ron and Linda the power of thought provided choices for them to make a difference in their relationship.

Know that when they talk about relationships they are referring to three categories:

1. As a couple (how you communicate with your husband/wife, boyfriend/girlfriend).
2. Yourself (how you communicate with you, are you in touch with your inner/outer self?).
3. Family (how you communicate with your family, do you spend some time, no time or all of your time with your family?).

Ron and Linda are Connecticut residents and are the proud parents of three wonderful children and two beautiful grandchildren.

www.ingramcontent.com/pod-product-compliance
Lightning Source LLC
Chambersburg PA
CBHW051435280526

45785CB00003B/1294